D0442631

"In cookie, there is strength."

—*Aesop*

SESAME STREET

[Imprint]
MAKE YOUR MARK

NEW YORK

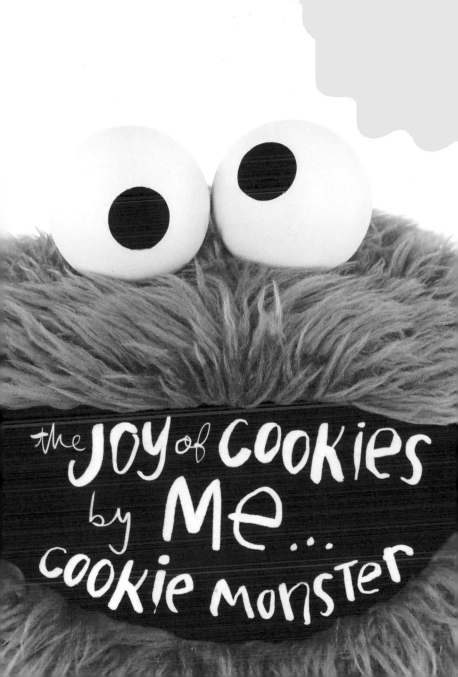

the JOY of COOKieS
by Me...
COOKie MonSTer

[Imprint]
MAKE YOUR MARK

A part of Macmillan Publishing Group, LLC
175 Fifth Avenue, New York, NY 10010

Library of Congress Cataloging-in-Publication Data is available.

ISBN 978-1-250-14341-9 (hardcover)

Our books may be purchased in bulk for promotional, educational, or business use. Please contact your local bookseller or the Macmillan Corporate and Premium Sales Department at (800) 221-7945 ext. 5442 or by e-mail at MacmillanSpecialMarkets@macmillan.com.

Special thanks to Julie Kraut

Imprint logo designed by Amanda Spielman

First edition, 2018

1 3 5 7 9 10 8 6 4 2

Me the only Cookie Thief in this here town.
So no steal cookies! And no steal book *about* cookies!
Or terrible cookie curse fall upon you:
Cookie forever taste like dust in mouth.
Fate worse than diet!

Me dedicate this book to me Grandma Monster.
She give me greatest gift of all: Love.
Also known as first plate of
MiLK and COOOOKiES!!!

INTRODUCTION

When me first decide to write book about cookies,
me . . . wait, cookies?

Me no can wait!
Me got to
HAVE COOK
COWAB

ES **NOW!**
UNGA!!

PART I

WHY COOKIES?

Me first idea was make book out of

COOKiES,

but early copies mysteriously . . . missing.

Cookie is like high five for stomach.

Who stole cookie from cookie jar?
Was it . . .

Okay, me.

OBVIOUSLY
iT ME.

How me eat cookies?
Let me count the ways:

One, open mouth.
Two, put in cookie.
Three, me confused. Three *cookies*?
Four cookies!!!! Oh, me so excited!

FiVe CookieS!

SiX CookI
SEVEN
EiGHT

COOKIE CRUMB of WISDOM

ME EAT COOKIE,
THEREFORE

ME
AM.

Let them eat cookie.
And let me eat cookie, too!

What's me favorite cookie?

COOKiE iN ME TUMMY!

IN CASE OF EMERGENCY, BREAK GLASS AND EAT COOKIE.

In case of serious emergency, eat two.

Me eat more than just cookies:
Me also eat fruit, vegetables, hamburgers, neckties,
cookies,
pasta, burritos, carpet, grandfather clock,
cookies,
chicken, sandwiches, shoes, telephones,
Stephen Colbert's Peabody Award, bicycles,

cookies,
tacos, cookbooks, hats, signs, kaleidoscope,
me TV remote control,

cookies...

MmMmm, coooookies.

What was me saying?

Only one good place for eating cookie.

EVERYWHERE!

No matter what they take from me,
they no take away cookie.

Because
ME EAT
iT!

Cookie jar
half full or half empty?

TRiCK
QUEStiON!

Me was here.
It completely empty, of course!

Now, ordinarily, me tell you
that me not going to eat this cookie.

But let's face facts . . .
me going to eat this cookie.

Me just one cookie away from being full.

ALWAYS.

COOKIE CRUMB *of* WISDOM

TO EAT COOKIES
OR
NOT TO EAT COOKIES...
THERE IS

NO

QUESTION.

DIAMOND IS FOREVER.

COOKIE IS FOR NOW.

C is for cookie,
that good enough for me!

Sorry, did me sing that out loud?

Letter M me second favorite letter.

is sound me make when me eat cookie!

Small cookie excellent appetizer for

BIGGER COOKIE.

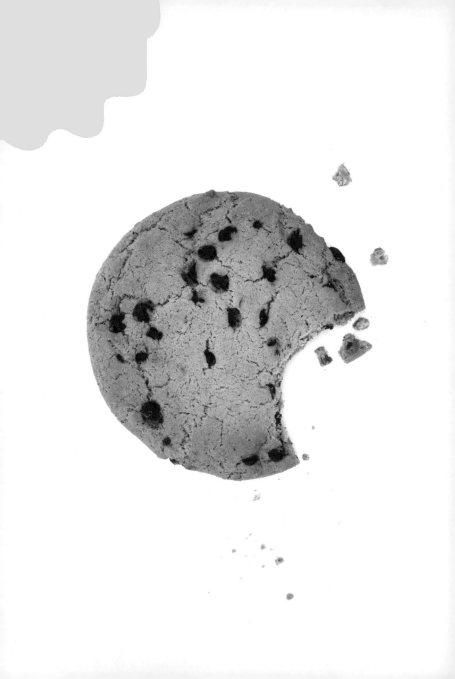

PART II

FOR LOVE OF COOKIES

Me just monster,
standing in front of cookie, asking it to . . .

OOPS, COOKIE GONE.

Me ate it.

If question going to be cookie,
answer going to be

YeS!

No matter what question is,

ANSWER iS COOKiE.

(Sometimes answer is love.

But always also cookie.)

Fill life with
PEOPLE YOU LOVE.

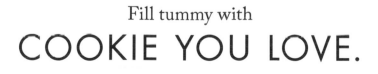

Fill tummy with

COOKIE YOU LOVE.

LOVE

is meaning of life.

LOVE COOKIES

is purpose of life.

COOKIE CRUMB *of* WISDOM

BE THE MONSTER YOUR COOKIE DESERVES.

In Dessert Olympics,

COOKIE DESERVE GOLD MEDAL!

Me secret ingredient for cookie is
LOVE.

And tiny bit of sea salt on top.

Home where heart is.
Heart where cookie is.
Math clear:
Home is cookie.

Love means never having to say mc sorry
. . . for eating last cookie.

But still, me sorry.

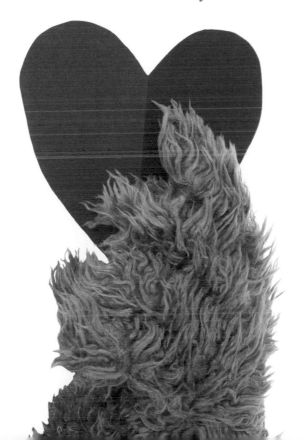

Ginger. Chip. Sugar.
Cookie by any other name would
still taste as sweet.

SO HELL CHIP!

ME FAMOUS COOKIE DOUGH

SUGAR COOKIES!

INGREDIENTS

¾ cup butter or margarine (soft, but not melted)

1 cup sugar

2 eggs

1 teaspoon vanilla extract

2½ cups all-purpose flour

1 teaspoon baking powder

1 teaspoon salt

Me make cookies come into existence before me very eyes. Me BAKE cookies! Yeah yeah yeah.

DIRECTIONS

1. Me put butter in mixing bowl.

2. Me put sugar in bowl.

2½. If me want *chewy chocolate chippy cookies*, me add ½ cup brown sugar here.

3. Me smoosh butter and sugar all together with fork or large spoon.

4. Me put in eggs and vanilla next.

5. Me smoosh more.

6. Me add flour, baking powder, and salt.

6½. If me want *chewy chocolate chippy cookies*, me add 1 cup chips here.

7. Me mush up everything with fork. Or spoon. Or hands. Me not picky.

ME NO EAT COOKIE DOUGH.

8. Me put cookie dough in refrigerator for 1 hour.

1 HOUR LOOONG TIME.

9. Me roll on floured surface. Cut cookie dough into tasty shapes. Move to ungreased cookie sheet.

STILL NO EAT COOKIE DOUGH!

10. Put in 400°F oven for 8 minutes.
    Maybe 10, if you like crispy cookie.

10 MINUTES

VERY

LOOOOOONG TIME.

OOOH,
COOKIES!!!

OM NOM NOM NOM NOM
NOM NOM

PART III

LIVE BEST COOKIE LIFE

LIFE SHORT.

Cookie at breakfast!

Breakfast most important meal of day,
if you have cookie at breakfast.

If you have cookie at lunch,
lunch most important meal of day.

Early bird gets worm.

But cookie taste better than worm.
SO ME SLEEP IN.

It always

COOKIE O'CLOCK

somewhere.

So many cookies. So little time.

Me need a cookie break.

Oooh,
no-cookies *soooo* hard!
Okay, okay, okay,
what should reward be for
no-cookie break . . . ?

Me know!
CoOKiES!

Me love smell of cookie in morning.
And afternoon.
And evening.
And when
me sleeping.
And when me dreaming,
and when me
wake up in
middle of the
night, and
WHEN

ME...

Sorry, me getting a bit carried away here.

Sometimes me dream me is carrot monster.

Then me wake up.

COOKIE CRUMB of WISDOM

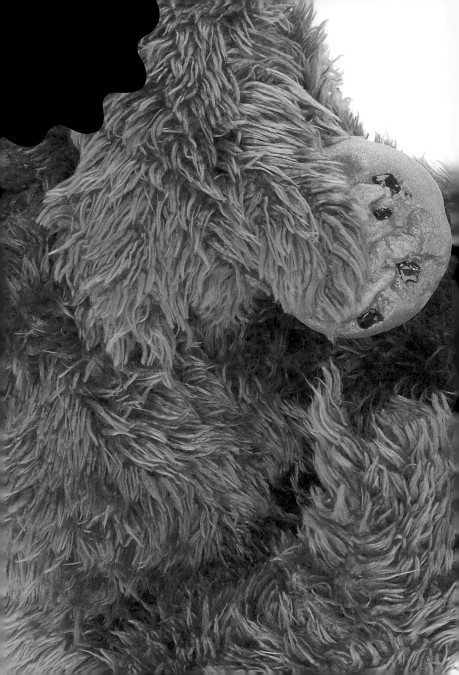

You cannot keep cookie
for later and also eat cookie now.

Unless you have . . .

TWO COOKIES.

Cauliflower . . .
or cookie?
Cauliflower . . .
or cookie?

ME COOKIE MONSTER!

This no-brainer!

You can lead monster to cookie jar, but . . .

WAiT, JUST LEAD MONSTER TO COOKiE JAR!

Sorry, no but.

Balanced diet is important.

For example, me eat chocolate chippy cookie.
Then me eat green leafy salad.

(*Then me eat oatmeal raisin cookie.*)

Cookie not diet because

COOKIE
IS
LIFESTYLE.

Also because
cookie not very good diet.

YOU
ONLY
LIVE
ONCE.

But if you eat enough cookies, once enough.

Me favorite cookie:

chocolate chippy

SNICKERDOODLE

MINT CHOCOLATE CHIPPY

OATMEAL RAISIN

BANANA OATMEAL

CHOCOLATE

toffee CHIPPY

crunch

CINNAMON CARROT

SWIRL CAKE

COCONUT RAISIN

PEANUT BUTTER

chocolate chocolate chippy

SALTED CARAMEL CHIPPY

GINGER
MOLASSES
white chocolate
SEA SALT LINZER
HOCOLATE CHiPPY THUMBPRINT
BACON
CHOCOLATE CHiPPY
peanut butter and jelly
ALMOND BUTTER DATE
DARK CHOCOLATE PiSTACHiO
CRANBERRY
caramel pecan

Me look at list and think:
Not enough cookies!

BODY
BY
COOKIE.

PART IV

MY COOKIE, MY FRIEND

EXHALE NEGATIVITY.

INHALE COOKIES.

COOKIE CRUMB of WISDOM

COOKIE IS AS COOKIE DOES.

And cookie does delicious!

Some say keep friends close but enemy closer.

ME SAY KEEP COOKIE CLOSEST.

Sometimes me think,
WHAT IS FRIEND?

And me think,
FRIEND SOMEONE YOU
GIVE UP LAST COOKIE FOR.

ME NEVER MET
COOKIE
ME NO LIKE.

But me also never formally introduced to cookie.

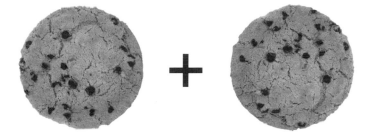

Two wrongs not make right.
But two cookies . . . make everything right.

Stranger just friend me have not
shared cookie with yet.

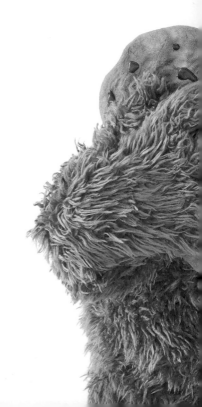

Me can eat cookies,

and me can eat cookies with friend,

but me cannot eat friend's cookies.

Also me cannot eat friend.

Who invent cookie?

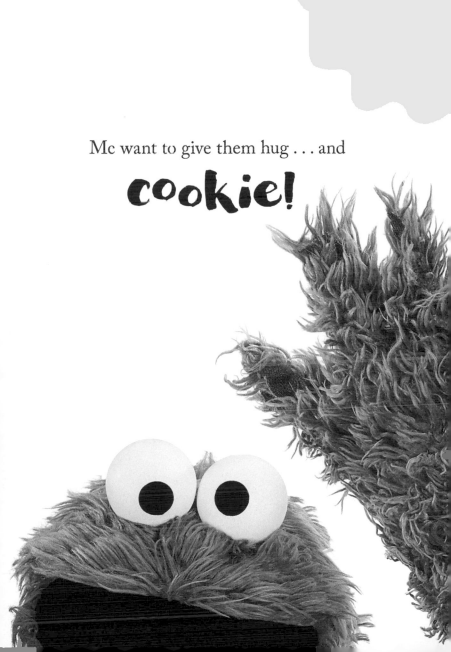

Mc want to give them hug . . . and

cookie!

Me think two types of monster in the world:
Monsters who love cookies and . . .

monsters who LOVE cookies

Sorry, me make mistake. Just one monster type.

~~monsters who~~
~~DON'T LOVE cookies~~

COOKIE CRUMB of WISDOM

ASK NOT
WHAT COOKIE
CAN DO
FOR YOU,

JUST
EAT
COOKIE!

NO TALK TO IT.

A good friend give you cookie.

A best friend give you
MANY COOKIES.

Me so hungry for cookies, me ate cookbook.
So many delicious cookies inside!
But not as tasty as real thing.

So now me going to make some *real* cookies.

All me need is recipe from cookbook.

Oooops!!!

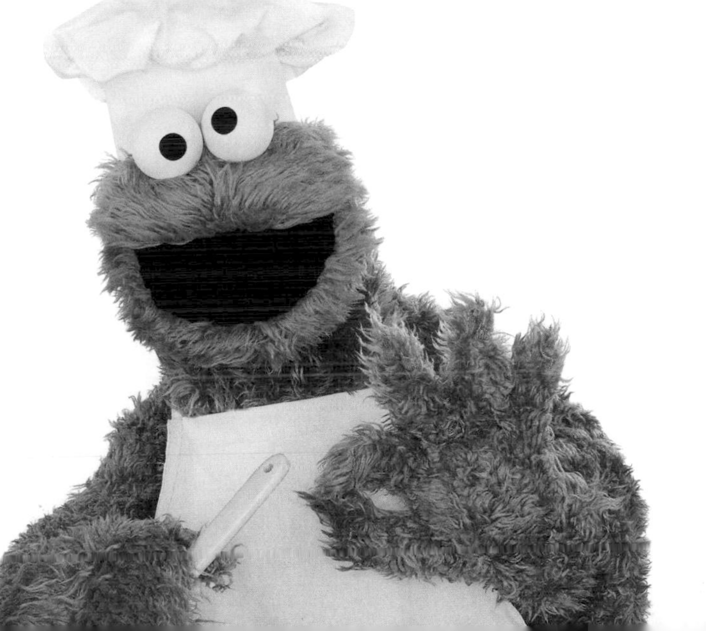

WHEN ME NEED CHOCOLATE

DOUBLE CHOCOLATE COOKIES

INGREDIENTS

DOUGH:

2 cups sifted all-purpose flour

1 teaspoon baking soda

¼ teaspoon salt

¼ pound (1 stick) butter

3 ounces (3 squares) unsweetened chocolate

1 cup dark brown sugar (pack firm)

1 egg

1 teaspoon vanilla extract

½ cup heavy cream

GLAZE:

1 ounce (1 square) unsweetened chocolate

1 tablespoon butter

1½ tablespoons hot water

2 tablespoons heavy cream

1 cup confectioners' sugar

GOT DOUBLE BOILER?
Oooh, me new recipe
pretty complicated.
BUT iT WORTH iT! Yeah.

CHOCOLATE!!
me say too much chocolate
but that impossible!

DIRECTIONS

1. Me preheat oven to 375°F.

2. Me grease baking sheets.

3. Me mix flour, baking soda, and salt and put to side.

4. Me cut butter into ½-inch chunks and put in heavy, 3-quart saucepan.

5. Me add chocolate. Cook over low heat until melted.

6. Me take chocolate off heat. With heavy wooden spoon, stir in sugar.

7. Me add egg and vanilla and stir until smooth.

8. Me stir in half of dry ingredients. Then me sloooowly stir in cream.

9. Me add remaining half of dry ingredients. Stir briskly until dough is all smooth.

10. Me drop heaping tablespoon of dough on cookie sheet one by one, at least three inches apart. Should make about 18 cookies.

SOMETIMES ME END UP WITH
LESS THAN 18 ... ME NOT SURE WHY.

11. Me bake 12–15 minutes. Or until cookies look spongy. But firm.

Me let cookies rest on cookie sheet, then on cooling rack.

While cookies cool, me make glaze.

12. In top of double boiler, me melt chocolate with butter.
13. Me remove top from heat. Add hot water, heavy cream. Stir.
14. Me add sugar and stir until smooth.
15. Me sometimes need to add more water or sugar. Make sure it feel like heavy cream sauce.
16. Me smooth glaze over cookie tops, careful to leave ½-inch clear all around cookie edge.

Somehow, me have to leave cookies alone for 1 hour.

WHILE ME WAIT, EYES GLAZE OVER.

Cookies so HYPNOTIZING!

MMM, COOKIES!!

OM NOM NOM NOM

NOM NOM

PART V

COOKIE TRUTHS

COOKIES

Making Mondays okay one bite at a time.

When life give me lemons,

me ask if anyone got recipe
for lemon cookies.

Cookie may not be solution to
ALL world's problems. But maybe?

ME THINK IT WORTH A TRY.

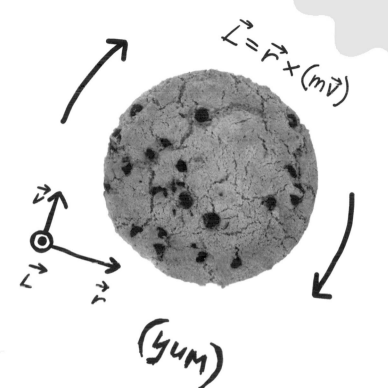

$$\vec{L} = \vec{r} \times (m\vec{v})$$

(yum)

COOKIE MAKE
WORLD GO ROUND!

Cookie and conservation of angular momentum.

Only thing between you and happiness
is lid to cookie jar.

Smile always just a cookie away.

Me heard cookie a day keep doctor away.
Whose idea only ONE cookie a day?

THIS VERY BAD ADVICE.

COOKIE CRUMB of WISDOM

SPEAK SOFTLY

SOFTLY

AND

CARRY BIG

COOKIE.

Big enough to share with good friend.

No cry because
COOKIE IS FINISHED.

Smile because
COOKIE HAPPENED.

Behind every successful monster
is empty cookie jar.

COUNT YOUR COOKIES,

not your problems.

Before me eat first cookie of day,
me
MONSTER.

After, me still monster.
But me
HAPPY MONSTER.

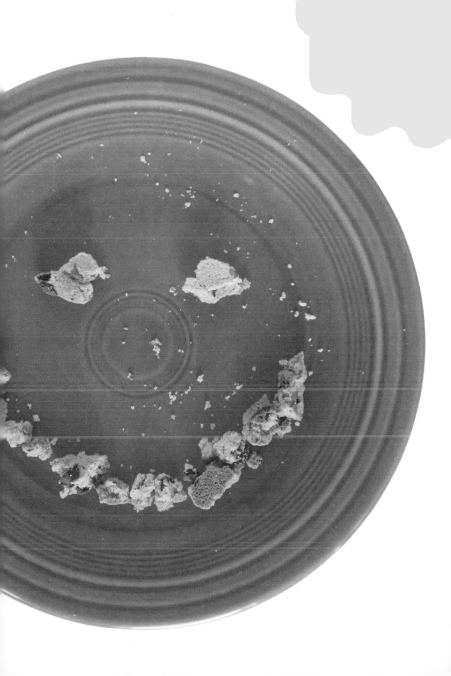

You cannot buy happiness,
but you can buy cookie.

AND COOKIE JUST AS GOOD!

Me not even sure what difference is.

IF SAD, EAT COOKIE.

If still sad, talk to doctor.
Sounds serious.

COOKIE CRUMB of WISDOM

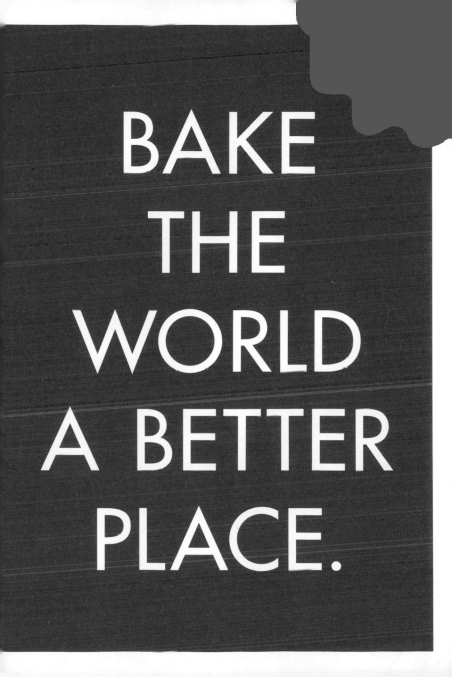

EVERY MONSTER DESERVE COOKIE

EVERY-MONSTER COOKIE

INGREDIENTS

⅔ cup coconut oil (or me can use vegetable shortening)

½ cup brown sugar

½ cup granulated sugar

1 teaspoon vanilla extract

¼ cup applesauce

1¾ cups oat flour

½ teaspoon salt

½ teaspoon baking soda

1 cup chocolate chippy of choice

NO nuts, NO dairy,
NO eggs, NO gluten!

DIRECTIONS

1. Me preheat oven to 375°F.

2. Me use parchment paper to line cookie pan so no crumbs to clean.

CRUMBS TO EAT!

3. Into first bowl, me measure coconut oil, sugar, vanilla, and applesauce.

4. Me stir all together with spoon (or mixer for shortening) until nice and squishy.

5. Into second bowl, me measure oat flour, salt, baking soda, and chocolate chippy.

6. Me stir until all dry stuff mix together.

7. Me pour dry-stuff bowl into wet-stuff bowl.

8. Me use spoon or mixer until everything all nice and creamy.

9. Me chill dough 30 minutes.

WHY? WHY???
iT SO HARD TO WAiT!!!

10. Me plop dough onto cookie pan with tablespoon.

YEAH YEAH YEAH

ALMOST COOKIES NOW!
ME CAN TASTE IT.

11. Bake 10–12 minutes. (Maybe 2–3 minutes longer
   if use shortening or if like crispier cookie.)

Keep close eye
on cookie.

12. Me share cookies with vegan monsters.

AND OTHER MONSTERS, TOO.

LIKE MEEEE!!!

COOOOKK
EEEEEEE!!

It okay to forgive self for eating cookies.
By eating cookie.

AUTHOR'S NOTE

Me hope you agree this very tasteful book.
And tasty.

OM NOM NOM NOM

NOM NOM

NOM NO

NOM

ACKNOWLEDGMENTS

Me would like to thank
the letter C and number 2.
Because two cookies
always better than one.

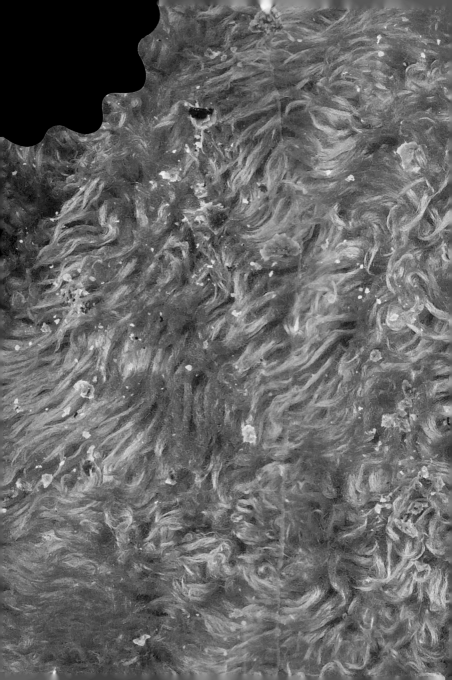